TIME
FOR KIDS
READERS

TO THE RESCUE

by Joanne Randolph

Harcourt
SCHOOL PUBLISHERS

Orlando   Austin   New York   San Diego   Toronto   London

Visit *The Learning Site!*
www.harcourtschool.com

Firefighters put out fires.

Firefighters rescue people.

Firefighters
teach us about
fire safety.

4

They teach us not to play with matches.

They teach us safe ways to get out of a building.

They teach us how to stop, drop, and roll.

stop **drop** **roll**

Now we know about fire safety.